All about BIRDS

THE ANSWERS TO THE QUESTIONS
YOU HAVEN'T THOUGHT ABOUT

Copyright © 2024 by WhyWhatHuh

All rights reserved.

No part of this book may be reproduced, distributed, or transmitted in any form or by any means, including photocopying, recording, or other electronic or mechanical methods, without the prior written permission of the publisher, except in the case of brief quotations embodied in critical reviews and certain other non-commercial uses permitted by copyright law. For permission requests, write to the publisher, addressed "Attention: Permissions Coordinator," at the address below.

2 Edition

Legal Notice:

While the author has made every effort to ensure the accuracy of the information contained in this book, the information is provided without warranty, express or implied. Neither the author nor the publisher shall be held liable for any damages caused directly or indirectly by the information contained in this book.

Hold fast to dreams, for if dreams die, life is a broken-winged bird that cannot fly.

Langston Hughes

CONTENT

Introduction 7
The WHATs 10

1. What clever trick do ravens use to get help from wolves, and are they planning a dinner party? 11

2. What makes flamingos pink, and how are shrimp part of their beauty routine? 13

3. What's behind a hummingbird's neat hovering trick? 15

4. What clever gadget do crows use to crack nuts, and could this be a hint at a crow takeover? 17

5. What bird takes more naps in the air than anything else? 19

6. What's all the chatter about when starlings flock together? 21

7. What's the only bird that flies backwards, and what's its cool secret? 23

8. What risky gift do penguins propose with? 25

9. What wild dance moves are birds of paradise known for? 26

10. What part of a bird can tell us its age like tree rings do for trees? 28

11. What's the tiniest bird in the world, and how does it keep warm? 30

12. What bird uses tools, and do they have tiny toolboxes? 32
    ### Myth Smashers 34

The WHYs 37

1. Why do flamingos stand on one leg, and is it a secret yoga move? 38

2. Why do penguins waddle instead of walk, and do they know how cute it is? 40

3. Why do crows hold grudges, and could you be on their naughty list? 42

4. Why do some birds travel thousands of miles, and are they ever jet-lagged? 44

5. Why do owls twist their heads around, and do they get dizzy? 46

6. Why is the cuckoo such a bad birdie, and is its bad name deserved? 48

7. Why do parrots mimic humans, and do they know what they're saying? 50

8. Why do some birds spruce up their nests, and are they the first decorators? 52

9. Why do peacocks spread their feathers, and does it really work? 54

10. Why do vultures like their meals sun-baked, and does it improve the taste? 56

11. Why do albatrosses stick together for life, and what's their secret? 58

12. Why have city birds turned into night owls, and do they have secret lives? 60

    Myth Smashers 62

The HOWs 65

1. How do penguins stay warm in the cold, and are their suits more than just stylish? 66

2. How do pigeons find their way home, and do they come with built-in GPS? 68

3. How do woodpeckers peck so much without headaches? 70

4. How do flamingos eat upside-down, and what's their dining trick? 72

5. How do some birds "sing" with their feathers, and why do they do it? 74

3 | WHY WHAT HUH?!

6. How do arctic terns manage their epic migrations, and do they ever go off course? 76

7. How do birds of prey spot prey from so far, and do they have super-sight? 78

8. How do ostriches run so fast without flying, and have they mastered speed-walking? 80

9. How do birds sleep while flying, and do they dream? 82

10. How do birds exchange secret messages, and can we learn from them? 84

11. How do lyrebirds mimic any sound, and is there a downside to this skill? 86

12. How do swifts spend all their lives flying, and do they need rest stops? 88

    Myth Smashers 90

The WHENs 93

1. When did birds start as dinosaurs, and how did they turn into the feathered flyers we see today? 94

2. When did the ancient bird-dino archaeopteryx first fly, and how did it manage? 96

3. When did humans start using pigeons for mail, and did the birds get lost? 98

4. When were birdhouses invented, and are birds picky about their homes? 100

5. When did Darwin study finches, and how did these birds change science? 102

6. When did Audubon begin drawing American birds, and did it take off like he hoped? 104

7. When did hummingbirds first head to the Americas, and were they welcomed? 106

8. When did passenger pigeons disappear, and why was it such a shock? 108

9. When did swans become love symbols, and did they choose this role? 110

10. When did bird-watching become a thing, and was it always trendy? 112

11. When were birds used in mines for danger alerts, and were they divas about it? 114

12. When did birds first start flying, and what sparked this big change? 116
   Myth Smashers 118

The HUHs 121

1. Huh?! Did you know some parrots have better rhythm than us, and do they wish for dance shows? 122

2. Huh?! Did you know the European pied flycatcher plans for climate change, and should we take notes? 124

3. Huh?! Can you believe chickens are kin to T. rex, and do they feel the pressure? 126

4. Huh?! Is it true pigeons know art styles, and are they secret critics? 128

5. Huh?! Did you know some birds "borrow" nests, and are they bad decorators? 130

6. Huh?! Did you know some birds sleep with one eye open, and do they dream of flying? 132

7. Huh?! Can you believe there's a bird that copies human laughter, and do they join in jokes? 134

8. Huh?! Did you know crows have funerals, and should we invite them to ours? 136

9. Huh?! Is it true some birds use ants as a spa treatment, and are they getting a free scrub? 138

10. Huh?! Did you know pigeons were war heroes, and do they have tiny medals? 140

11. Huh?! Did you know some birds see magnetic fields, and are we missing something? 142

12. Huh?! Did you know the lyrebird copies construction sounds, and are they adding to urban noise? 144

Myth Smashers 146

Introduction

Welcome to the feathery world of "All About Birds," where every flap and chirp hides a surprise! Get ready to dive into the extraordinary lives of our winged friends. Ever wondered if ravens and wolves are up to something more than just dinner plans? Or if penguins know how cute they look when they waddle? Perhaps you're curious about the birds that manage to nap mid-flight. This book is here to uncover these mysteries and more.

Why do flamingos get their pink glow from shrimp? How do woodpeckers keep pecking without splitting headaches? And would you believe some parrots can outdance us? From the ancient flights of archaeopteryx to the unique songs of feathered musicians, this book is packed with amazing facts that will change how you see our avian pals.

Short and sweet: crows use tools. Long story: lyrebirds mimic just about anything. Every chapter unfolds a new story of bird magic, from clever tricks to wild antics. So, get ready to spread your imagination and soar into the quirky, curious skies of bird wonder!

9 | WHY WHAT HUH?!

The WHATs

Faith is the bird that feels the light when the dawn is still dark.

- Langston Hughes

1. What clever trick do ravens use to get help from wolves, and are they planning a dinner party?

Ravens and wolves might not seem like obvious dining buddies, but these unlikely pals have a clever trick up their feathers and fur—a collaboration that feels like they're planning a wild dinner party. But don't worry, there's no RSVP needed, and the menu is strictly nature's buffet, not a gourmet spread.

Ravens are incredibly smart birds, often called the "feathered apes" of the animal world because of their problem-solving skills. They also have a knack for mimicking sounds, like those funny videos of birds imitating ring tones. Their true smarts, though, show in how they work with wolves. Picture this: a raven spots a carcass and sends out a call, almost like saying, "Hey, wolves, dinner's over here!"

Now, why bother inviting wolves? Ravens have sharp eyes from above but lack the tools to tear into tough animal hides. Wolves, with their powerful jaws, are perfect for opening up a meal that ravens can't manage on their own. By calling in the wolves to do the hard work, ravens get a tasty share once the wolves have had enough. In return, wolves get the benefit of the raven's keen eyesight to find food they might miss. It's a win-win, the ultimate "you help me, I help you."

What's really interesting is how ravens seem to get the value of this partnership. They even show off playful moves, like diving and swooping, to keep the wolves interested. It's like they're jesters making sure their audience is entertained and ready for the feast.

So, while it might look like ravens and wolves are planning a grand forest feast, it's really a smart survival strategy. It's nature's way of showing us how life is connected in surprising ways. Sometimes, the lessons on working together can be right under your beak or snout, waiting to be discovered.

2. What makes flamingos pink, and how are shrimp part of their beauty routine?

Flamingos are nature's runway stars, flaunting their striking pink outfits. But instead of visiting a salon, they get their vibrant color from a rather unusual source: their diet.

So, what's on the menu? Algae and tiny critters like shrimp. These snacks are loaded with carotenoids—the same pigments that make carrots orange. When flamingos gobble them up, these pigments are transformed inside their bodies, painting their feathers pink. It's a bit like how eating lots of carrots might give your skin a healthy tint, but for flamingos, it's all about the style.

Carotenoids are like their personal beauty products, turning dull gray chicks into fabulous adults. Without these, they'd be as plain as a rainy day. But with them? Stunning.

Think of shrimp as little bottles of flamingo blush. They're not just a part of the flamingo's diet; they're the highlight of it, giving them that show-stopping color.

So next time you see a flamingo, remember—they're strutting their stuff with a diet rich in aquatic snacks.

You really are what you eat, especially when your meal plan includes shrimp with a splash of algae!

3. What's behind a hummingbird's neat hovering trick?

Hummingbirds, the tiny helicopters of the bird world, have nailed the art of hovering with a skill that would make the best drones jealous. Imagine if you could just hang out in mid-air, sipping nectar as if it were the finest juice, all while flapping your wings up to 80 times per second. Pretty cool, right?

The secret behind this hovering magic is in their wings and flying style. Unlike most birds that flap their wings up and down, hummingbirds move theirs in a figure-eight shape. This clever move creates lift on both the upward and downward flaps, keeping them hanging in the air. It's like a never-ending workout—but from nature's gym.

Hummingbirds have supercharged little hearts and a sky-high metabolism to power all this flapping. Their hearts can beat over 1,200 times a minute! To keep up with their busy lifestyle, they gulp down lots of sugar, visiting hundreds of flowers a day. They're basically a sugar rush on wings.

Their sturdy chest muscles, making up about 30% of their body weight, give them amazing control. They can zip in every direction—even backward. Wouldn't reversing the car be easy if we could do that?

When you watch a hummingbird hover, it's like seeing a high-energy dance put on by tiny performers. Next time you spot one of these little flyers, take a moment to enjoy their air show. These mini marvels remind us that the sky's the limit—especially when you can hover like a pro.

4. What clever gadget do crows use to crack nuts, and could this be a hint at a crow takeover?

Crows, those clever black birds of the sky, have a knack for solving problems that would impress even the most tech-savvy humans. Their tool of choice for cracking nuts isn't some fancy new invention but something surprising—traffic.

Picture a crow sitting on a streetlamp, a walnut in its beak. Instead of struggling with the tough shell, the crow drops the nut onto a busy road. The cars do the hard work, cracking it open. Once the traffic lights turn red and the cars stop, the crow swoops down to grab its treat. Smart, right?

Scientists have noticed this clever trick. It shows that crows aren't just using tools—they're also good at understanding how things work and have a sense of timing. These are not just bird-brained actions; they are signs of true intelligence. In the animal world, this is rare and really impressive. It's what you might call urban smarts.

Could this mean a crow takeover? Probably not. While their smarts earn them respect (and sometimes a wary glance from humans), crows are more likely to cause a bit of harmless fun than to rule the world. For now, they're happy watching us, waiting to grab a snack when they can.

Next time you spot a crow by a crosswalk, remember: they're not just hanging around. They might just be outsmarting us in the puzzle department. Let it be a reminder that sometimes, the simplest solutions are right in front of us—or, in this case, right under our tires.

5. What bird takes more naps in the air than anything else?

In the world of napping champs, the alpine swift soars to the top, taking more naps in the air than anything else. This bird is a true high-flyer, snoozing while gliding thousands of feet up. Imagine napping without missing out. It's like enjoying both cake and clouds at once.

Scientists, using tiny tracking gadgets, found that these swifts can stay in the air for up to 200 days without landing. During this epic flight, they manage to nap mid-air. How? By switching off half their brain at a time. This neat trick lets one side rest while the other stays alert, like a built-in autopilot.

The secret to their aerial naps lies in their build. Their sleek bodies and long wings make them perfect for effortless gliding. They don't just rest for fun—it's a must. Their diet of flying insects keeps them moving. Landing for a nap? Not really an option.

While we wrestle for comfort on bumpy flights, the alpine swift glides along, peaceful yet watchful. It's a reminder. Life's best moments sometimes come not from sitting still, but from staying on the move. Even if that means napping on the go. Next time you crave a cozy nap spot, think of the alpine swift, the true master of sky-high siestas.

6. What's all the chatter about when starlings flock together?

When you see starlings flocking together, it might seem like they're having a giant birdie gossip session, chatting about the latest worm-finding tips or critiquing last season's messy feathers. But really, you're watching a stunning show called a "murmuration." It's like a flash mob, but with wings and way more style.

Why do these little chatterboxes gather in such mesmerizing clouds? Besides looking impressive enough to make pigeons feel a bit plain, starlings murmurate mainly for protection. It's a classic case of "safety in numbers." By flying together, they confuse predators like hawks and falcons. Imagine trying to catch a single popcorn kernel in mid-air at the movies, but they're all popping at once. That's what it's like for the predators.

There's more to their airborne meet-up than just dodging becoming dinner. Starlings are naturally social. These gatherings are like an evening catch-up before they settle down for the night. They might be swapping vital info, like where the best food is or which trees offer the warmest places to sleep.

The science behind their flying routine is fascinating, too. Think of it as a perfectly choreographed dance, without a leader yelling, "five, six, seven, eight!" Each bird keeps an eye on six or seven neighbors, adjusting speed and direction to match. This amazing coordination is known as "scale-free correlation." You won't need that term for trivia night, but it's good to know!

Next time you see a murmuration, don't just wonder if they're plotting something big. Realize you're seeing an incredible natural spectacle. It balances beauty, survival, and a splash of social interaction. It's nature's way of showing that sometimes, chatting with friends really can save your life.

7. What's the only bird that flies backwards, and what's its cool secret?

In the world of birds, where feathers are fancy and flying is top-notch, one tiny creature stands out with a unique trick. It's a bird that can fly backwards! Say hello to the hummingbird, nature's own ace pilot.

Hummingbirds are like the busy bees of the bird world. While most birds just flap and glide, hummingbirds have a special talent—they can hover like a miniature helicopter. Their wings flap up to 80 times a second, letting them fly backwards and pull off slick moves like zipping sideways or stopping mid-air. A drone would be envious!

How do they do it? The secret is in their shoulder joints. Not a gym workout, but a special ball-and-socket joint gives them a full range of motion. This nifty trick allows backward flight and swift turns. They are like buzzing athletes on a sugar rush.

Their tiny hearts can beat over 1,200 times a minute when flying. Imagine that! To keep up with this high-speed lifestyle, they need lots of energy. They drink sugary nectar, making them the ultimate sweet-loving flyers.

Next time you see a hummingbird, remember you're watching one of nature's best flyers. They break the rules of flight with style, proving that sometimes bending the rules leads to the coolest tricks. Keep flying, little backwards bird, and keep amazing us with your sky-high stunts!

8. What risky gift do penguins propose with?

When it comes to proposing, penguins have a unique way to pop the question. Meet the "penguin proposal," which involves a pebble—not just any pebble, though. It's a carefully chosen, perfect stone. Penguin couples, especially the Adelie and Gentoo types, use this small rock as a symbol of partnership.

Why risk everything on a rock? The answer is both clever and practical. These pebbles help build nests. In the chilly lands where these penguins live, the right pebble keeps the eggs safe and warm, off the icy ground. A sturdy nest boosts their chances of raising a family, making the pebble a high-stakes gift indeed.

Finding the perfect pebble is filled with drama. Sometimes, penguins resort to "pebble theft," sneaking stones from nearby nests if the beach's supply runs low. It's survival of the smartest, adding a bit of adventure to their romance.

So, the penguin's pebble proposal is both practical and poetic—a real rock-solid promise to build a life together. Next time you fret over choosing a gift, remember: even penguins feel the pressure. They just handle it with a twist of flair and a splash of risk on the ice!

9. What wild dance moves are birds of paradise known for?

In the dense, magical jungles of Papua New Guinea, the birds of paradise are not just winged wonders—they're the unrivaled stars of the dance floor. Forget ballroom or salsa; these feathered dancers have mastered moves that would make human performers jealous.

Imagine this: a male bird of paradise, sleek and dazzling, sets the stage. Using his vibrant feathers like a colorful scarf, he kicks off his performance. The moves? Think Michael Jackson's moonwalk, a touch of Broadway flair, and some surprising breakdancing. Some species unfurl their feathered capes or spread out their fans like umbrellas, swaying and hopping with energy that would put any nightclub to shame. The Lesser Bird of Paradise is famous for its bobbing and weaving, while the Blue Bird of Paradise does a sideways slide that could steal the show on any competition.

But these moves aren't just for fun. They serve a big purpose: catching the eye of a mate. The females, acting as judges in this dance-off, have a keen eye for creativity and charm. The male's routine needs to be perfect—one wrong move, and he might end up dancing solo. Scientists tell us it's all part of sexual selection, where the best dancers pass on their dazzling traits.

What's really amazing is the evolution at play here. These birds have developed such wild routines because their environment is safe and rich in resources. This means more time to charm and less time to worry about food or danger. It's like living in a neighborhood so safe, you can spend your days perfecting your dance moves instead of stressing over dinner.

So, next time you think about nature's dancers, remember the birds of paradise. They show us that sometimes, the best way to stand out is to break the mold, maybe even add a little twirl. After all, when it comes to the art of attraction, isn't it better to just wing it?

10. What part of a bird can tell us its age like tree rings do for trees?

Birds don't come with a "best before" date stamped on them, but their feathers can spill some surprising secrets about their age. Think of them as nature's version of a diary, each feather telling a tale. When a bird molts—losing old feathers to grow new ones—these fresh feathers hold clues to the bird's life story.

Understanding this is all about looking at the wear and tear of feathers. Young birds start with feathers that look a bit rough around the edges, like they just survived a vigorous game of tag with Mother Nature. As they transition to adulthood, they lose these rookie feathers for a sleeker set. These new feathers often look smoother and more colorful, marking the bird's move into grown-up territory.

In some birds, the hints are even clearer. Just like an avian mood ring, certain birds show changes in color and pattern as they age. Take the American Robin, for example—its spots disappear as it matures. Or the European Starling, whose beak shifts from brown to yellow as it gets older.

Ornithologists, the scientists who adore birds, act like feather detectives. They examine wear, check for "molt limits" (those are lines where old and new feathers meet), and note any color changes. Through these clues, they can estimate a bird's age with a surprising level of accuracy.

So, while birds don't add years by growing rings, they do wear their age on their sleeves—or rather, their wings. Next time you spot a sparrow fluffing its feathers, remember: those quills might just be the closest thing to a birth certificate. Isn't nature's design just marvelously clever?

11. What's the tiniest bird in the world, and how does it keep warm?

Meet the bee hummingbird, the smallest bird on Earth! This tiny champ from Cuba weighs less than a dime and could curl up inside a teacup, if it wanted to. At just about 2 inches long, it makes even the word "lightweight" seem heavy.

But here's the big question: how does such a small bird stay warm in a world that can be pretty chilly? Well, the secret lies in some clever tricks and a serious knack for staying cozy. First off, these birds have a super-fast metabolism. Think of it like drinking 150 cans of soda a day just to keep moving—that's what these little birds do, flitting from flower to flower, sipping nectar as if it's rocket fuel.

When night rolls around, and nectar stops flowing, they pull off a neat trick. They enter something called torpor. It's like a mini hibernation. Their body temperature drops, and their metabolism slows right down, saving energy and keeping them warm. It's like turning down the thermostat without raising the heating bill.

And if that's not enough, these birds come with an awesome set of feathers. They trap air, making a snug little layer that keeps them cozy, just like a puffy jacket. Despite their tiny size, bee hummingbirds have the art of staying warm all figured out. They show us that great things come in small, feathery packages. So, next time you shiver, just think: if a bird the size of a jellybean can handle the cold, you can too!

12. What bird uses tools, and do they have tiny toolboxes?

Tool use among birds might sound like a scene from a cartoon, with feathered friends carrying tiny toolboxes. Imagine them with miniature hammers and screwdrivers! In reality, nature spins an even better tale, especially with the clever New Caledonian crow.

These birds are the MacGyvers of the bird world. They don't lug around hardware, but they do make tools from twigs, leaves, and even feathers. Their favorite trick? Crafting hooks to snag tasty insects hiding in hard-to-reach places. Picture a person using a bent wire to fetch a lost key from a drain. That's the crow in action! These birds are so skillful that scientists have devoted entire studies just to figure out their smarts.

But how do these feathery engineers pick up such a talent? They're not just winging it. New Caledonian crows have fantastic problem-solving skills. They also learn by spotting tricks from other crows, a bit like an internship. Only here, there's less coffee and more cawing involved.

And while it might let down some that these birds don't have actual toolboxes strapped to their legs, their tool-using skills are truly amazing. It makes one wonder what they could achieve with a full DIY kit. Perhaps one day, we'll see crow-built nests that rival fancy penthouses.

In the end, the New Caledonian crow's talent for tool-making shows that even in the animal world, creativity knows no limits. So next time you struggle with assembling IKEA furniture, remember: there's a crow out there who might just do it better!

Myth Smashers

✖ **MYTH:**

If you touch a baby bird, its parents will abandon it.

✔ **FACT:**

Most birds have a limited sense of smell and won't recognize your scent. They won't mind you helping a chick; in fact, they'll likely continue caring for their young. Just as a parent recognizes their child in a crowded playground, bird parents know their chicks by sight and sound.

✖ **MYTH:**

Birds will explode if they eat rice.

✔ **FACT:**

The idea that rice causes birds' stomachs to burst is unfounded. Birds can safely eat uncooked rice, similar to grains they find in the wild. The act of tossing rice at weddings won't harm birds any more than feeding them seeds.

The WHYs

No bird soars too high if he soars with his own wings.

- Rabindranath Tagore

1. Why do flamingos stand on one leg, and is it a secret yoga move?

Flamingos are like the yoga experts of the bird world. If they wore yoga pants, they'd probably be all over Instagram. Their cool one-leg pose isn't just for looks—this funky habit actually has a purpose.

Scientists have puzzled over why flamingos love standing on one leg. A popular idea is that, much like us, they enjoy being warm. By tucking one leg up, they save heat, which is super helpful when they're wading through cold water looking for their next meal. Imagine eating seafood while keeping one foot out of freezing water—no thanks!

But there's more. Balancing on one leg gives their muscles a break. Flamingos are designed so that standing on one leg uses less energy. Ever tried holding a yoga pose too long and felt the burn? Flamingos have figured out how to stay chill with minimal effort.

Interestingly, this pose is more common when flamingos are just hanging out, in their version of bird Netflix and chill. If they're awake and active, they switch it up, using both legs like us.

So, while flamingos might not be dishing out secret yoga tricks soon, their one-legged act is both a clever way to stay warm and a smart energy-saver. Nature's flamingo ballet is both practical and graceful—showing us that sometimes, keeping balanced is the best move.

2. Why do penguins waddle instead of walk, and do they know how cute it is?

Penguins, those dapper little residents of the icy South, have a waddle that could outdo any toddler's adorable march. But why don't they just walk like other animals?

Imagine this: penguins are built like tiny submarines. Their short legs are set far back on their bodies, perfect for gliding through water but not for striding on land. When they need to move on solid ground, they shift their weight from side to side, giving us that famous waddle. It may look clumsy, but here's the clever part: it's actually a very energy-efficient way to get around on snow and ice without falling over. Who knew clumsiness could be so smart?

Now, do penguins realize how cute they are? Probably not. They likely don't understand our swooning over their frosty runway walks. But if there was a bird pageant, they'd certainly strut with pride, oblivious to human standards of beauty.

Next time you watch these feathered wonders waddle, remember: it's not just for laughs. It's nature's crafty design, dressed in a cozy coat of Arctic charm. Imagine if humans waddled too—our sidewalks would be seas of swaying bodies, and fashion shows would become a whole new spectacle!

3. Why do crows hold grudges, and could you be on their naughty list?

Imagine a world where birds could hold grudges like people do. For crows, that's not just science fiction. These brainy birds are known for their sharp memory and brains, and they aren't shy about using these skills to their advantage—or perhaps to your disadvantage.

Crows are part of the corvid family, famous for being super smart. They solve puzzles, recognize themselves in mirrors, and make tools from twigs. But here's the kicker: they also have a talent for grudge-holding.

Studies show that crows can remember human faces. At the University of Washington, researchers wearing masks caught and tagged crows. What happened next was like a bird version of a neighborhood watch: whenever someone donned one of those masks again, the crows went berserk, dive-bombing and scolding them. And this wasn't just a flash in the pan—it went on for years. Talk about a long memory!

Why do they do this? It's mostly about survival. By remembering who's a threat and warning each other, crows boost their chances of staying safe. Many animals do this, but crows? They take it to a whole new level.

So, could you be on a crow's naughty list? If you've ever given a crow a hard time—or just looked shady to them—you might be. But here's the silver lining: crows can forgive, especially if you make things right. Try winning them over with peanuts or other treats; after all, the way to a crow's heart might just be through its stomach.

Whether you're on a crow's bad side or not, it's a testament to these amazing birds' memory and smarts. Next time you spot a crow, give it a friendly nod. You never know when you might need a bird buddy—or just want to keep on their good side.

4. Why do some birds travel thousands of miles, and are they ever jet-lagged?

Some birds have an itch that can only be scratched by flying thousands of miles. Their epic trips, known as migration, are journeys like no other. But why do these feathery adventurers take such long flights, and do they ever face a bird version of jet lag?

First, the big "why." Birds migrate mainly to find food and a safe spot to raise their young. As seasons change, so do food supplies. Many fly to warmer places where there's plenty to eat—like flying to a never-ending buffet. Imagine a seasonal all-you-can-eat bird feast.

Now, how do they navigate? Birds don't use GPS, but they do have an internal compass. The sun, stars, and Earth's magnetic field guide them. Some scientists even think they might follow scents across continents. Talk about a true sense of adventure!

And now, to the question that's been pecking at your mind: Are they jet-lagged? Birds aren't quite like us in that way. They don't zap through time zones like we do. Instead, they take it slow and steady, with stops along the way. Think of them as nature's marathon runners, pausing to rest and snack before hitting the sky again.

Take the Arctic Tern: it flies around 44,000 miles a year from the Arctic to Antarctica. Meanwhile, the Bar-tailed Godwit makes non-stop flights over the ocean for days. These feats are so impressive, you might think these birds have frequent flyer miles.

While we endure cramped airplane seats and bland meals, birds make travel look easy. Their journey is instinct-driven and focused on survival. So, the next time you see a V-shaped silhouette in the sky, remember: these birds might not know jet lag, but they've truly mastered the art of the long-distance commute. Maybe they even have some tips for us on handling travel with style and grace.

5. Why do owls twist their heads around, and do they get dizzy?

Owls are like the gymnasts of the bird world, twisting their heads in ways that would make yoga teachers jealous. But why do they do it? It all comes down to their eyes and a bit of quirky biology. Unlike us, owls can't move their eyes around. Those big, round eyes are stuck in place—like two bright flashlights. So, to look around, they have to twist their whole head. And here's the amazing part: they can turn it up to 270 degrees. Try looking behind you without moving your shoulders, and you'll start to get the picture.

You might wonder if all this head-spinning makes owls dizzy. Surprisingly, it doesn't. Owls have a clever setup. They have 14 neck bones (we have just 7), and a unique system of blood vessels keeps blood flowing to their brains even during all that twisting. It's like having an internal safety harness, keeping things steady while they check out their surroundings.

In the animal world, being able to literally watch your back gives these night-time hunters a big advantage. So, while we might turn our heads with less drama, owls show us that looking at life from different angles can be useful—even if it means a bit of neck-stretching.

47 | WHY WHAT HUH?!

6. Why is the cuckoo such a bad birdie, and is its bad name deserved?

The cuckoo, it seems, has quite the reputation as the bird world's troublemaker—a real feathery rascal. This bad-boy image comes from its unique approach to parenting, or lack thereof. Instead of building its own nest, the cuckoo sneakily lays its eggs in the nests of other unsuspecting birds. It's like hiring a nanny and never coming back. Clever, right?

But why does the cuckoo do this? For starters, it saves a ton of energy. No need to waste time on nest-building or chick-rearing. All its effort goes into laying more eggs and finding more nests to crash. While birds like warblers and pipits might find this a bit cheeky, from the cuckoo's perspective, it's just good parenting strategy.

The cuckoo's trickery doesn't end there. By making its eggs look like those of the host birds, it pulls off a great disguise. The host birds, not exactly known for their detective skills, usually end up raising the cuckoo chick as their own. And here's the kicker: once hatched, the little cuckoo often pushes the other chicks out, ensuring it gets all the attention and food. That's one ambitious chick!

Is the cuckoo really a "bad" bird? Maybe that's a bit unfair. It's just doing what it knows best in the game of survival. In some places, its antics even keep nature's balance in check. It's a funny twist in the circle of life.

So, does the cuckoo deserve its bad name? Perhaps not. Let's tip our hats to its clever survival skills. In the grand tale of nature, the cuckoo isn't a villain—it's just a bird with some smart tactics and a knack for surviving. Who doesn't love a good hustle now and then? The cuckoo isn't bad; it's just got the best parenting hack in the wild.

7. Why do parrots mimic humans, and do they know what they're saying?

Parrots, those chatty birds, have a talent for mimicking humans that can either make us laugh or scratch our heads. Picture a pet that almost orders pizza for you—not quite reality yet, but let's uncover why they repeat our words and if they understand their own chatter.

In the wild, parrots live in noisy groups where talking is super important. Mimicking is their secret tool to blend in, kind of like a tourist picking up local slang but with feathers and a love for sunflower seeds. It's their way of saying, "Hey, I'm part of the squad," even if the squad is a human saying, "Pretty bird!"

But do parrots really know what they're saying? Here's where it gets interesting—or a bit like a parrot trying to tell a joke. Parrots don't understand language like we do. They link words to certain reactions or rewards. So when Polly says, "Hello!", Polly might just want a bit of attention or a tasty snack rather than contemplating greetings.

Some smarty-pants parrots, like African Greys, might use words a bit more wisely. Think of Alex the African Grey—he was like the Einstein of birds. He learned over 100 words, knew colors and shapes, and seemed to get ideas like same and different. So, while most parrots are like sound recorders, a few might just play the role of a tiny professor.

In the end, parrots mimic not because they're mini linguists but because they're social and love connection. Whether they're serenading you or just squawking for a cracker, they remind us that talking isn't just about words—it's about being understood. Even if it's by a beak and a bobbing head. Next time your parrot squawks "Good morning," know it's not just talking. It's joining a delightful dance of friendship. Who'd have thought chatting with a bird could be so wonderfully complex?

8. Why do some birds spruce up their nests, and are they the first decorators?

Some birds seem like they've peeked into a decorating handbook, picking just the right twig or fluff to make their nests both snug and stylish. This might make you wonder if these feathered architects were the first decorators, even before humans spruced up their caves. But the reasons behind their nest decor aren't just about having an eye for design.

Birds dress up their nests for many reasons, blending necessity with clever showmanship. For some, adding certain bits and bobs is like a personal ad for mates. Much like humans might flaunt a flashy car or a well-stocked bookshelf to impress a date, birds use nest decorations as a feathered billboard. Male bowerbirds, for example, are known for their fancy nests filled with colorful objects to catch a female's eye. They've got an egg-cellent sense of style!

But it's not always about showing off. Sometimes, it's pure practicality. Some birds line their nests with aromatic herbs thought to repel pesky parasites, keeping their young safe. Think of it as birdie air freshener—a natural way to keep bugs away and make the nest smell like a bird spa. Others might use special materials to help stay warm or hide from the bad guys.

While birds may not have invented interior design, they've been at it for millions of years, long before we ever hung a cave painting. Their nest decorating shows us that beauty isn't just skin-deep; it can be useful and key for survival.

In the end, whether it's about love or being smart, birds remind us that decorating goes way back. So, next time you plump your pillows or rearrange your room, think of our feathered friends with their evolutionary flair. They prove that a sprinkle of creativity can mean life, feather, and love.

9. Why do peacocks spread their feathers, and does it really work?

Peacocks are like the pop stars of the bird world—flashy, flamboyant, and always ready to wow the audience with their stunning feather shows. But why do they spread those big and beautiful feathers? It's all about attracting a mate and putting on a bit of a show.

The main reason peacocks fan out their feathers is to impress potential partners. In nature's grand performance, the peacock's plumage is like a bright sign saying "Choose me!" The brighter and more eye-catching the feathers, the better the chance of winning over a peahen. Scientists call this sexual selection. The idea is that a peacock with striking feathers is showing off how healthy and strong he is—the kind of guy you'd want to pass genes onto the next generation.

And yes, it really works! Studies show that peahens are indeed drawn to the peacocks with the most stunning feathers. It's as if they have a natural sense of style. But the peacock's tail isn't just a splash of color; it's like an evolutionary ad, finely tuned over ages to catch a peahen's discerning eye.

There's even more to this feathered show. As a peacock spreads his tail, he also creates low sounds, known as infrasound. These sounds can add an extra touch to the visual display, offering a bit of an audio-visual experience. Seems like peahens enjoy a full show, like a dinner date with both lights and music.

But carrying around that tail is not without its problems. It's heavy, making it hard to run away from predators. Imagine trying to sprint with a huge parachute on your back! Yet, the peacock's tail is a perfect example of evolution's balance between staying alive and catching a mate.

In the end, while the peacock's tail might seem a bit over-the-top, in the world of romance, showing off can be very effective. Whether bird or human, sometimes you've got to pull out all the stops to get noticed. So next time you see a peacock strutting his stuff, remember: he's not just showing off—he's playing the game of love, bird-style.

10. Why do vultures like their meals sun-baked, and does it improve the taste?

Vultures aren't known for fancy dining, but their taste for sun-baked meals is quite curious. These birds seem to favor their food like a hot roadside snack, served up by the sun. But what's with this sunbathing preference? Does it really make dead animals tastier?

To solve this riddle, we need to think beyond flavor. Vultures, with their bald heads and sharp eyes, have a practical reason for liking their meals warmed by sunshine. It's less about fancy flavors and more about hygiene. When a carcass sits in the sun, the heat acts like nature's oven, slowing down bacteria growth. This is key for vultures, even though their super-strong stomach acids can handle some nasty stuff. They still prefer a meal with fewer bacterial surprises.

The heat also softens the meat, making it easier for vultures to tear apart with their sharp beaks. Think of the sun as a natural tenderizer. For vultures, this means less wrestling with tough meat and more dining time. And that's crucial when other birds are eyeing the same meal from above.

But does this sunny process improve taste? Probably not. Vultures aren't picky about flavor. They're more about being smart and safe. Their great sense of smell leads them to food, but the sunbaking is all about efficiency, not spice.

In the end, vultures master the art of turning not-so-great food into a sensible meal. With the sun as their cooking partner, these birds make the most of what nature offers. So, when you spot a vulture enjoying a sunny snack, remember: to them, the sun isn't a garnish—it's part of the recipe!

11. Why do albatrosses stick together for life, and what's their secret?

Albatrosses, those majestic ocean flyers, seem to hold the secret to lifelong love. These seabirds are famous for sticking with one partner for their entire lives, suggesting they might know a thing or two about lasting relationships—or at least some top-notch teamwork.

The reason for their commitment is pretty practical: raising chicks is hard work. Albatrosses mate for life to give their young the best shot at survival. With their giant wings, which can stretch over 11 feet, they need lots of energy for flying to and from distant nests. By working together, they share the load, ensuring there's always a parent around to protect and nurture their chicks.

So, what makes albatrosses such experts at long-term partnerships? It starts with their courtship rituals, which are all about bonding. Imagine dance routines that would outshine a ballroom contest, paired with synchronized grooming sessions. These activities help albatrosses pick the right partner and build a strong bond.

Once they're together, albatrosses maintain their relationship through trust and support. They take turns on long migrations, sit on eggs, and search for food. That's commitment—making even the most dedicated human couples seem lazy.

Scientists think part of their secret is in their nature. Albatrosses can live over 60 years, giving them plenty of time to nurture their love. Plus, they usually lay just one egg every year or two, so they can't afford to spend ages looking for new mates.

In short, albatrosses show us that teamwork, talking, and shared goals help raise strong chicks and keep love flying high. Maybe we should take notes: a little dancing, lots of patience, and remembering that sometimes, two wings are better than one.

12. Why have city birds turned into night owls, and do they have secret lives?

City birds have traded their morning chirps for moonlit tunes, turning into unexpected night creatures. It's almost like they've joined a secret club, just for those with feathers. But why are they swapping dawn for dusk, and what are they up to at night?

Let's peek into the busy life of a city. Cities are always alive—full of traffic sounds, bright lights, and the occasional honking orchestra. In this noisy setting, daytime might not be the best time for a bird to be heard. So, urban birds are turning to the night. The quiet helps their songs travel farther, letting them chat and flirt without competing with the city's racket.

And then there's the city nightlife itself. Even after sundown, street lights keep things bright, and this helps birds see well enough to hunt and flit about. Lights attract insects, turning them into easy snacks. Nighttime dining, anyone?

Do these birds have secret nighttime lives? While we haven't caught them at late-night jazz gigs or secret meetings, the switch to night life is a big change.

Some, like the European robin, have even reset their internal clocks to enjoy the quieter hours. They've adapted to urban life, making the night their new stage.

Think of city birds as smart musicians. They plan their shows when there's less noise, making sure they're heard. They've adapted cleverly, making the most out of city living.

So, next time you hear a bird singing to the stars, remember this: it's not just serenading the night but thriving in the urban jungle. And who knows? Maybe they're keeping a little nighttime mystery tucked under their wings.

Myth Smashers

✕ MYTH:

All birds fly south for the winter.

✓ FACT:

Not all birds migrate. Many species have adapted to stay put, finding food and shelter in colder climates. Think of city pigeons; they're happy staying in one place year-round, just like some bird species in the wild.

✕ MYTH:

Birds rely solely on feeders and will starve if feeders are empty.

✓ FACT:

While feeders are a treat, birds are resourceful and adept at foraging naturally. They may visit your backyard for a quick snack but have multiple sources, much like visiting different cafes for coffee.

The HOWs

The reason birds can fly and we can't is simply because they have perfect faith, for to have faith is to have wings.

- William Blake

1. How do penguins stay warm in the cold, and are their suits more than just stylish?

Ever seen a penguin waddling around and thought, "Nice tuxedo, but isn't it a bit cold for formalwear?" These birds aren't just the fashionistas of the animal world; they're survival experts in Antarctica's deep freeze. How do they do it? Clever biology and a few extra tricks that could make any human designer envious.

Let's start with those snazzy suits. Penguin feathers are not your typical bird attire. They're short, densely packed—over 100 feathers per square inch. Imagine wearing hundreds of coats layered together. These feathers form a waterproof barrier, keeping the icy seas at bay. Beneath this feather armor lies a thick layer of blubber, acting like a thermal blanket, trapping heat and blocking out the cold.

And when it comes to staying warm, penguins are professional huggers. Really. They huddle in big groups, pulling off the ultimate group hug to save heat and block those harsh winds. It's like a giant, feathery get-together where the only thing passed around is warmth.

Now, what happens when they dive into freezing water to catch fish? That's where their blood circulation comes into play. Penguins have a neat system called counter-current heat exchange. Warm blood flowing out from their hearts meets cold blood returning from their feet, warming it up before it circulates back. This way, they keep their insides warm even when their toes are chilling in icy waters.

In short, while penguins might look dressed for a gala, their style is all about practicality. Their suits aren't just stylish, but an evolutionary wonder designed for survival in harsh conditions. So next time you see a penguin, give them a nod of respect for mastering the art of looking fabulous while beating the cold.

2. How do pigeons find their way home, and do they come with built-in GPS?

Pigeons, those everyday grey birds gobbling crumbs at the park, have a hidden talent: they can find their way home from hundreds of miles away. No, it's not a fairy tale. It's real. These winged navigators don't have a GPS installed (no tiny antennas sticking out), but they have something just as cool.

Scientists aren't entirely sure how pigeons pull this off, but they've uncovered some clever tricks these birds have up their wings. To start, pigeons might have a thing for Earth's magnetic field. They sense the planet's magnetism with tiny iron bits in their beaks, much like a built-in compass.

But there's more to this story! Pigeons have amazing visual memory. They remember landmarks and use these mental snapshots to find their way. Think of it as having a mental map of their home turf. They also have a sense of smell that, while not as powerful as a dog's, can help them pick up familiar scents on their journey.

And just like your friend who swears by a shortcut, pigeons are flexible when navigating. They use the sun's position to guide them and have even been spotted following roads and highways—a feathered road trip, if you will.

Next time you see a pigeon nodding at you, remember you're looking at a skilled explorer. One that's got more orienteering skills than many humans. These birds show us that nature's simple tech can outsmart our fanciest gadgets. Who needs GPS when you're a pigeon with the perfect toolkit for adventure?

3. How do woodpeckers peck so much without headaches?

Woodpeckers are the rock stars of the bird world. With their non-stop drumming on trees, they're the ultimate percussionists. But how do they avoid headaches? You'd think all that pecking—up to 20 times a second—would leave them dizzy. Yet, the woodpecker's secret isn't tiny bird-sized painkillers. It's all about smart design.

First, let's talk about their heads. Their skulls aren't just hard. They're like nature's version of a high-tech helmet. This helmet has a special spongy bone structure that spreads out and dampens the force of each peck. Think of it like wearing a helmet lined with cushions: it turns a sharp hit into a gentle tap.

Next is their beak. It's strong yet flexible. The top and bottom parts aren't the same length, which helps spread out the force, keeping it away from their brains. This means each hit is more like a gentle knock than a painful thud. Their beak design is genius.

Inside that skull, the woodpecker's brain sits snugly, like an egg in a carton. It's small and tightly packed, minimizing movement and reducing the risk of any brain bashing. Plus, their neck muscles are super strong, which helps stabilize their head and soak up impact.

And here's the kicker: their tongue. This unique tool wraps around their skull, acting like a safety belt for their brain. It adds extra stability and cushioning. It's a clever design that keeps everything in place.

So, woodpeckers can keep on with their tapping without needing a break. Next time you hear that rhythmic tapping, remember: it's not just noise. It's a perfectly played tune backed by brilliant engineering. With nature as their guide, these birds prove that sometimes, the best solutions are right in front of us. Who needs a hard hat when you've got a built-in one?

4. How do flamingos eat upside-down, and what's their dining trick?

Flamingos are like the yoga masters of the bird world. They eat upside-down with more grace than a circus acrobat. But how exactly do they pull off this dining trick? It's all about their beaks. These birds have a special way of eating that would make any buffet lover jealous.

Picture this: a flamingo dips its head underwater. Its upside-down beak acts like a sieve and a straw. Flamingos feast on tiny treats like shrimp and algae. Their beaks are lined with ridges—a bit like a spaghetti strainer. These ridges help filter out mud and water, keeping the tasty bites inside. They do all this with their mouths while looking fabulous in their pink feathers.

Now, here comes the star of the show: the tongue. It works like a little piston. Flamingos suck water in, and the tongue pumps it out. This pushes the food against those ridges. It's a constant cycle of sucking and filtering. All this happens while they put on a show of water ballet.

You might notice flamingos with their heads at odd angles. For them, it's just part of the routine—no neck pain involved. Plus, the shrimp they munch on are full of carotenoids—the stuff that makes carrots orange. These turn flamingos' feathers that famous pink. Dining with a view and a fashion statement!

In the end, flamingos show us that sometimes flipping things upside-down leads to the best results. So, next time you hit a buffet, think like a flamingo. Just maybe skip the head-dipping part.

5. How do some birds "sing" with their feathers, and why do they do it?

In the bird world, singing is usually done the old-fashioned way: beaks open, tunes flowing. But some birds prefer a different approach, crafting melodies with their feathers. Take the club-winged manakin from South America's thick forests. Instead of using their voices, these birds create sound by rapidly clacking their wings together, like a drummer at a wild concert.

The magic of this feather music comes from a unique wing design. The club-winged manakin has special feathers that vibrate at high speeds—up to 100 times per second! This produces a sound similar to a violin played by an over-caffeinated musician. Not every bird can pull off this stunt. It requires special wing feathers that are tough enough to handle the intense shaking without wearing out.

Why go through all this effort when normal singing works for most birds? The answer is simple: love. In bird romance, it's important to stand out. By adding a musical twist to their courtship, these birds boost their chances of attracting a mate.

So, next time you hear the rustle of feathers making music, remember: in the search for love, some birds are willing to wing it with all they've got.

6. How do arctic terns manage their epic migrations, and do they ever go off course?

Arctic terns are the top travelers of the bird world. Each year, they fly an amazing 44,000 miles round trip from the Arctic to the Antarctic. These little birds somehow manage this huge journey, all without a GPS or a map-reader complaining about wrong turns.

Their secret? An incredible built-in toolkit for navigation. Arctic terns use the Earth's magnetic field, the sun's position, and even the stars to find their way. It's like they've got their own internal compass and sky map, making them the bird version of a savvy world traveler.

Their journey is anything but dull. Instead of a straight line, they weave a zigzag path over the oceans. Picture them like expert road-trippers, taking breaks at perfect spots to snack and rest, much like gathering frequent flyer miles in nature. It's all about eating well and dodging danger.

Do they ever go astray? Sometimes, yes. Strong winds and climate changes can nudge them off course. Yet, their navigation skills are so sharp that they're quick to find their way back. When they veer off, it's more like a scenic detour than getting truly lost.

In the end, the arctic tern's journey showcases nature's genius and their own adventurous spirit. They're like the Ernest Shackleton of birds, minus the tea and biscuits. So, next time you miss a turn on the way to the store, remember the arctic tern. A little zigzag can be perfectly normal—and even lead to an epic adventure!

7. How do birds of prey spot prey from so far, and do they have super-sight?

Birds of prey might not wear capes, but their eyesight is almost heroic. How do they spot dinner from dizzying heights? Well, let's dive into their super-sight.

For starters, these feathery hunters have eyes that are huge for their size. Imagine if we humans had eyes as big—that'd be like having grapefruits stuck to our faces. Their big eyes are full of light-sensing cells, giving them sight so sharp that your fancy TV seems like an old clunker in comparison.

Now, let's talk about their fovea, the secret weapon in their eyes. This part of the retina acts like a zoom lens. Some raptors even sport two foveae per eye, offering both wide and close-up views. It's like having birdy binoculars built right in, helping them spot even the tiniest mouse or fish, no matter how far away.

And colors? They've got a special talent there too. Their color vision is amazing, with a UV filter that's nothing short of magical. It helps them track UV-reflective trails left by rodents, like following a glowing breadcrumb path to a rodent lunch.

Curiously, their eyes are fixed—no rolling those peepers around. But fear not! Their necks can twist an impressive 270 degrees, like nature's own swivel cams. This means they can take in the whole scene without missing a trick.

So, do birds of prey have super-sight? Absolutely. They're like flying avengers of nature, scanning the skies with ease. Makes you wonder: if we had hawk-like vision, how many times would we find our keys without the couch-cushion chaos?

While we're left squinting up at the sun, these sky patrols are always on the lookout. So next time you glance upward, remember: they might be watching you with a clarity we can only dream of.

8. How do ostriches run so fast without flying, and have they mastered speed-walking?

The mysterious ostrich seems to have taken one look at its wings and decided, "Flying? No thanks! Running is way cooler." These birds are the track stars of the animal world, zipping across Africa at speeds up to 45 miles per hour. That's faster than a moped and with way more flair.

But what makes them run like the wind? First up, their legs. Think Usain Bolt, but with feathers. Ostriches have long, strong legs equipped with special tendons that work like springs. They store energy with each step and release it, letting them take strides as long as 16 feet. Picture yourself jumping over two basketball hoops in just one leap. Impressive, right?

And their feet are streamlined for speed. Just two toes per foot, with one big, claw-like toe leading the charge. This design cuts down on drag and makes them super fast on land. It's like having custom running shoes right out of the egg.

But don't forget—they've also nailed speed-walking. Their wide hips and flexible joints help them keep moving with a cool swagger. Perfect for dodging predators or just showing up fashionably late.

So, while ostriches won't be in the skies any time soon, they've got ground speed nailed. Next time you're racing an ostrich, remember: you're faster than a tortoise. But when it comes to running, enjoy the view from behind!

9. How do birds sleep while flying, and do they dream?

Navigating the skies while catching some sleep might sound tricky, but for some birds, it's just another part of their flying routine. Curious how they do it? Imagine alpine swifts and frigatebirds gracefully soaring through the sky, grabbing a quick nap mid-flight. But how do they manage to snooze without taking a nosedive?

The secret is in their amazing brains. Birds can sleep with one side of their brain at a time, a nifty trick called unihemispheric slow-wave sleep. This lets them keep one eye open for danger while the other side rests. It's like having your cake and eating it, too—resting while staying alert. Clever, right?

Now, do birds dream? Are they imagining endless fields of worms or epic sky adventures? While we can only guess if they're dreaming about their next wormy feast, birds do have a sleep phase similar to our REM sleep, known for dreams. Scientists have noticed brain activity in sleeping birds that looks a lot like what happens when we dream. So, while birds might not be scripting a feathered version of a Shakespeare play, it's likely something dream-like is going on.

So, next time you see a bird soaring across the sky, think about this: it might just be on a dream journey, navigating the clouds while half asleep. Now that's flying by the seat of its birdy pants!

10. How do birds exchange secret messages, and can we learn from them?

Birds, those chatty, feathery folks of the sky, have been swapping secret messages long before humans thought of secret codes. But how do they do it, and can we crack their feathery messages?

Imagine a world where you don't need WhatsApp or smoke signals—just the sweet sound of tweets and chirps bouncing between trees. Birds have nailed the art of sneaky talk, using songs, calls, and even moves to share messages. It's like their own version of Morse code and pretty smart at that.

Take the nightingale's song. It's more than a nice tune to fall asleep to. These notes are carefully crafted messages, often about turf or attracting a partner. Think of it as a love song with superpowers. What's amazing is that birds tweak their tunes depending on the situation—like changing from pop to rock when they're feeling bold.

Birds also talk with their bodies. The flashy dance of a bird of paradise could outdo any TikTok star. It's a dramatic way to show they're ready to find a mate or to claim their space. In everyday life, quick wing flaps or tail wags can mean danger or a nearby predator. It's bird semaphore, signaling a warning faster than you can shout "hawk!"

So, what can we learn? Birds show us that subtlety is key—how a small change in tone can flip a message. Their skill to change how they talk based on what's happening around them is something we could really work on. In our noisy digital world, maybe we should take a hint from our feathered pals: sometimes, saying less actually says a whole lot more.

In short, birds are nature's secret agents, mastering their hidden messages with flair. We might not start tweeting our conversations, but next time you hear a bird call, remember—there's probably more to that tweet than you think. So keep listening. You might just pick up a thing or two from the sky's secret service.

11. How do lyrebirds mimic any sound, and is there a downside to this skill?

Lyrebirds are the amazing voice impressionists of the animal world. These birds can copy almost any sound they hear, from the sweet songs of fellow birds to the loud buzz of a chainsaw. Picture living somewhere your alarm clock might suddenly sing like a car horn or your favorite tune might be whistled by a bird. Quite the show, right?

So, how do they do it? The magic happens in the syrinx, a special vocal tool at the base of a bird's throat. Most birds have a basic one, but lyrebirds have an extra-flexible, two-part syrinx. This gives them a huge range of sounds to play with. Imagine having a voice as flexible as a Swiss Army knife, ready to mimic any sound that comes along.

But, like all great skills, there's a catch. Sometimes lyrebirds get so wrapped up in copying sounds that they confuse potential mates. A lyrebird might sing a lovely mix of sounds, only to throw in the awkward noise of a camera click. Their talent could also turn into a noise nightmare if they live near a busy construction site.

In the wild, their ability to mimic anything can sometimes backfire. Yet, in today's ever-changing world, maybe being able to "sing" both sides of the soundtrack is a smart survival trick. After all, who wouldn't want to be nature's DJ, spinning the sounds of the forest and beyond?

12. How do swifts spend all their lives flying, and do they need rest stops?

Swifts, those amazing flyers of the sky, live lives that make our days look about as exciting as a game of rock-paper-scissors. Imagine spending almost your whole life in the air! These birds have mastered the art of constant flight, taking "frequent flyer" to new heights.

Swifts can stay airborne for months without stopping. They eat, drink, and yes, even sleep, all while flying. How do they do it? Their sleek bodies and long, curved wings let them glide smoothly, using very little energy. They almost never have to flap their wings. Instead, they ride the air currents, staying up with hardly any effort.

Eating is a breeze for swifts. They snag insects mid-flight—like grabbing popcorn during a movie, just without the greasy fingers. When they're thirsty, they skim over water surfaces, sipping as they glide by.

Sleep is where things get really clever. Swifts rest one side of their brain at a time while flying. This neat trick, called unihemispheric sleep, lets them nap without dropping from the sky. Talk about multitasking!

But even swifts need to land sometimes. During the breeding season, they return to solid ground to build nests and raise their chicks. Once the new swifts are ready, it's back to the skies.

So, while swifts might not need a rest stop, they show us that with the right wings, the sky's not just the limit—it's home. Remember: even though swifts might skip the rest area, they sure make the most of a snack bar in the sky!

Myth Smashers

✗ MYTH:

Owls can spin their heads in a full circle.

✓ FACT:

Owls possess remarkable neck flexibility, but they can only turn their heads about 270 degrees. This is enough to cover their surroundings thoroughly, just like an owl-like security camera with a wide field of vision.

✗ MYTH:

Penguins fall over when looking at planes.

✓ FACT:

Penguins are well-balanced and won't lose their footing just by looking up. They navigate icy terrains with ease, much like humans watching planes without tripping over their shoelaces.

The WHENs

We think caged birds sing, when indeed they cry.

- J.M. Barrie

1. When did birds start as dinosaurs, and how did they turn into the feathered flyers we see today?

Imagine if your Thanksgiving turkey had a distant, scaly ancestor that could roar louder than a lion at a prehistoric karaoke night. That's pretty much the story of birds. They began their journey during the Mesozoic era, when dinosaurs—rather than pigeons—were the ones making all the noise on Earth.

About 150 million years ago, some dinosaurs decided to try out a new look. These trendsetters started growing feathers. Not just any feathers, but ones that worked like a Swiss Army knife. They kept them warm, helped them show off to potential mates, and eventually gave them the ability to glide and fly. Meet Archaeopteryx, a creature caught between being a bird and a dinosaur, like a teenager unsure about their identity. It had wings, yet also teeth that definitely wouldn't win any dental awards today.

As time marched on, evolution made some clever tweaks. Bodies got sleeker. Flight muscles became stronger. Bones were reduced or fused together. These changes turned birds into the flying pros we see today, ready to hop between trees or travel across continents.

Evolution went a bit wild with colors and patterns too. It crafted everything from the plain but practical sparrow to the flashy peacock, which clearly ignored any advice about blending in.

In short, birds are the descendants of dinosaurs that grew to love feathers and flight. They left behind many of the traits of their heftier relatives. So, the next time you see a pigeon strutting about, remember: it's the low-key heir of some really impressive ancestors. Who knew dinosaurs were such fashion icons?

2. When did the ancient bird-dino archaeopteryx first fly, and how did it manage?

Picture this: 150 million years ago, during the late Jurassic period. Dinosaurs of all sizes are stomping around like they own the place. Among them, our feathery friend, the archaeopteryx, is getting ready to take its first flaps. It's like a bird and a dino mashed up together—a real prehistoric remix!

Now, scientists are still scratching their heads over how this creature managed to fly. Its feathers were definitely designed for flight, but its flying might have been more like a clumsy glide than a majestic soar. Imagine an ancient paper airplane with feathers. Not quite an eagle, but definitely aiming high.

With these wings, archaeopteryx probably used short flights. Escaping predators? Check. Catching prey? Absolutely. Flaunting those fancy feathers? You bet. Its lightweight bones and strong wishbone were perfect for all that flapping and hopping. It could run, jump, and flap its way into the air, a bit like a kid with new sneakers.

Why wings in the first place? Some say they were for showing off—picture a peacock mixed with a parrot, strutting in Jurassic style. Others think wings were handy for running or climbing trees. Evolution, though, had a better idea. Flying turned out to be pretty cool.

So next time you see a bird flying, think of archaeopteryx. It all started with this little creature taking a brave leap into the unknown. Who knows, maybe it invented the world's first 'birdbrain' idea of flight!

3. When did humans start using pigeons for mail, and did the birds get lost?

Pigeons delivering mail might sound like something from a quirky cartoon, but these feathered messengers have a long and fascinating history. The use of pigeons as mail carriers, known as "pigeon post," dates back to ancient times. Both the Greeks and Persians realized something remarkable about pigeons: their amazing ability to find their way home over long distances.

Here's how it worked: homing pigeons have an incredible talent for returning to their nest from faraway places. They use environmental clues, an innate sense of direction, and maybe a bit of pigeon magic. To send a message, someone would take a pigeon from its home, attach a tiny note to its leg, and release it. The pigeon, eager to get back to its cozy home (and probably some tasty birdseed), would fly straight back with the message.

But did these birdy mail carriers ever lose their way? Well, like any messenger, pigeons had their challenges. Weather could be a real problem, disorienting these sky posties. Predators, too, were scary threats. Even the bravest pigeon might rethink its flight path when facing a hungry hawk. Despite these hurdles, pigeons were known for their dependability. During both World Wars, these tough little flyers played key roles when other communication ways failed.

Despite some occasional missteps, pigeons paved the way for the high-tech communication we use today. Next time your text or email is late, just imagine a pigeon trying to find its way through a storm!

In the end, while tech might have taken over, pigeons as post workers remind us that sometimes, a little bird can carry a lot of weight—or at least a tiny note.

4. When were birdhouses invented, and are birds picky about their homes?

Birdhouses might not have the fame of the wheel or sliced bread, but they've been around for ages. Some of the first birdhouses appeared in the 15th century in Turkey. They weren't just shelters; they were fancy little artworks attached to buildings. These tiny homes were as much about kindness as they were about creativity.

Now, let's chat about birds and their picky tastes in homes. They can be choosy little things. In the world of bird real estate, location and home style matter a lot. Different birds desire different things: some like a snug space, others want room to stretch, and there's always one bird insisting on a scenic view. Take bluebirds, for instance. They love open spaces with not much clutter. On the flip side, wrens are like city dwellers, happy with a tiny spot just about anywhere.

Humans might fuss over paint colors and kitchen styles, but birds look for safety and easy food access. So, crafting a perfect birdhouse means getting the materials and style just right. If you do, you'll see birds lining up like they're at a new brunch spot.

But wait, there's more. Birds sometimes choose the most unexpected places for their nests. A forgotten shoe in the garage, a gap in the roof, or even an old watering can could be the next sought-after bird condo. If a family of sparrows decides your shed is their dream home, it's a compliment. They've checked out your space and decided it's worth moving in.

In the end, birds, with their historical roots and choosy nature, teach us something. While humans might obsess over curb appeal, birds keep it simple and practical. They pick their homes wisely, showing us they're perhaps the smartest real estate agents around, even if their focus is on survival rather than style. Plus, they come with the bonus of a cheerful morning song.

5. When did Darwin study finches, and how did these birds change science?

Picture this: it's 1835, and Charles Darwin is on a boat. Not just any boat, but the HMS Beagle. It takes him to the Galápagos Islands, where he meets some unusual bird buddies—finches. These small birds, with their different beak shapes and sizes, end up telling a story that changes how we see life on Earth.

Darwin didn't have a light-bulb moment right away when he saw the finches. He didn't drop everything and shout, "Evolution!" Nope, he collected these birds, made notes, and went on with his trip. But back in England, as he looked closer, he noticed something: the finches' beak differences weren't just random. These tweaks helped them fit right into their island diets.

This was the starting note to a big idea—natural selection. The finches showed that species can change, adapting to what they eat and where they live. It's nature's way of giving them an upgrade. Before long, these birds became the stars of Darwin's groundbreaking book, "On the Origin of Species," published in 1859.

The finches taught us more than just science. They taught us about being curious—how small things can lead to big ideas. Like those finches, science keeps changing. Who knows what the next discovery might teach us about life? In the end, the finches remind us that sometimes, birds of a feather don't just flock together—they think outside the nest.

6. When did Audubon begin drawing American birds, and did it take off like he hoped?

In the early 19th century, a man named John James Audubon took on a colorful mission that was both ambitious and eye-catching: to draw every bird species in America. This wasn't just a casual stroll in the park with a pair of binoculars. Armed with a paintbrush and a huge passion for birds, Audubon started this lofty project around 1820.

At first, his paintings were about as popular as yesterday's leftovers. American publishers showed little interest, not unlike a cat's indifference to vegetables. But Audubon wasn't easily ruffled. He packed up his bird portraits and headed to England in 1826, hoping for better luck across the Atlantic.

And lucky he got! His life-sized illustrations, called "The Birds of America," were a sensation. They dazzled with vibrant colors and fine details. Soon, British patrons couldn't get enough. Audubon's fame spread quicker than a startled flock of pigeons. His work didn't just take off—it truly soared, turning him into a legend of both bird studies and art. Today, his art is more sought after than the last piece of cake.

Audubon's story shows you that sometimes chasing your dreams can lead to views from the treetops. A journey that's quite for the birds—in the best way possible.

7. When did hummingbirds first head to the Americas, and were they welcomed?

Imagine this: millions of years ago, a tiny feathered explorer set off on an epic journey. The destination? The Americas. But this wasn't your typical vacation plan. Hummingbirds started this great migration from Europe and Asia. They landed in the Americas around 22 million years ago.

Picture these lively little birds zipping through lands shared with prehistoric giants. They didn't have a map or a plan. It was about survival, a bit of evolution, and a sprinkle of luck.

Were they welcomed? Well, that depends. Prehistoric bugs might have felt less thrilled, suddenly finding themselves on the dinner menu. But the plants? Different story. They had a party. Hummingbirds and plants struck up a deal—hummingbirds got all the nectar they could drink, and plants got their pollen spread far and wide. A perfect handshake, or should we say wingshake?

For us humans, these nectar-loving guests have become more than just pollinators over time. With their sparkle and incredible flying tricks, hummingbirds have dazzled us. They've become symbols of joy and wonder, showing us that even the smallest creatures can make a big impact.

So, were hummingbirds rolled out a welcome mat in the Americas? Nature sure did, with flowers aplenty. And we? We've embraced them as tiny marvels of nature, albeit ones with a bit of a sweet tooth. In the grand adventure of life, their journey to the Americas was truly a soaring success.

8. When did passenger pigeons disappear, and why was it such a shock?

The passenger pigeon, once so numerous they could eclipse the sun, vanished on September 1, 1914. The last of them, a bird named Martha, took her final rest in a Cincinnati zoo. Think of passenger pigeons as the rock stars of the bird world, with their numbers once hitting an unbelievable 3 to 5 billion across North America.

Their sudden disappearance was like discovering your favorite band broke up overnight. What went wrong? It was a mix of human ambition and pigeon predictability. With the telegraph and railroads, hunters tracked these birds with ease, turning their massive flocks into a grand buffet. It was like the pigeons were waving a big sign that read "Eat me!"

Their living quarters vanished too. As forests turned into towns and farms, their hangouts disappeared quicker than you can say "logging." Plus, they weren't great at adapting. Passenger pigeons were social creatures; they needed big groups to get in the mood for romance. Smaller numbers meant much less mingling and more lonely evenings.

This extinction was a big wake-up call. It taught us that even the most common creatures can disappear if we don't take care of our world. A lesson in humility wrapped in feathers: what we do matters, and it matters a lot. So while Martha's tale is a bit sad, it left us pondering how to live alongside nature without wiping out another species. Wouldn't it be nice if the only thing disappearing in flocks were our worries?

9. When did swans become love symbols, and did they choose this role?

Swans have been on quite the romantic journey through history, earning their reputation as symbols of love. But did they ever get a say in this, or did we just decide it for them?

Let's take a peek into mythology. The ancient Greeks were smitten with swans. Imagine Zeus, king of the gods, turning into a swan to woo a human queen, Leda. That certainly raised the bar for romance! Swans were sacred to Aphrodite, the goddess of love. She probably gave them the role because, let's face it, turtles just aren't as romantic.

Fast forward a few centuries, and swans are still at it. In literature, Shakespeare often used them to symbolize purity and beauty. They became the star couple of the natural world. But why?

Swans are mostly monogamous. They mate for life. Or at least until someone new and more feathery comes along. Their lifelong partnership turned them into symbols of loyalty and love. Picture them, gliding together on peaceful waters—humans couldn't help but think, "If only our relationships were that smooth."

But do swans actually know they're love symbols? Probably not. They're more focused on finding the best nesting spots and defending their turf. Yet, their charming behaviors—neck-entwining, synchronized swimming, team-building—keep reinforcing their romantic image.

In the end, while swans didn't exactly apply for the role of love's symbols, they've played it beautifully. Maybe they got a nod from the gods, or maybe their elegant moves just charmed us all. Swans are now the ultimate symbol of love. And who knows? Maybe deep down, they enjoy the spotlight.

10. When did bird-watching become a thing, and was it always trendy?

In the timeline of hobbies, bird-watching—or "birding" as insiders call it—is a relatively new pastime. It only really spread its wings in the 19th century. Before then, people mostly paid attention to birds for practical reasons, like figuring out which ones might make a decent meal or a comfy pillow.

The bird-watching buzz really began in Britain during the Victorian era. With factories popping up everywhere, folks started craving a bit of nature. Armed with new bird books and some hefty binoculars, early birders went out to spy on our feathered friends. Think of it as the 1800s version of a Netflix marathon, just with more fresh air and fewer spoilers.

But was bird-watching always trendy? Not exactly like today's viral dance moves. In the Roaring Twenties, snapping a photo of a rare bird was just as thrilling as catching a jazzy dance number. Fast forward to the post-war years, and bird-watching became a suburban staple. It was the activity that brought grandparents and kids together long before social media ever did.

Today, bird-watching is having a major comeback. It's hipper than a trendy owl with glasses. As people become more aware of the environment, birding offers both peace and a thrill. Now, birders can use apps like eBird to share their sightings, turning their bird-spotting into important data for science.

So, was bird-watching always in style? Maybe not like the latest dance craze, but it's been quietly flapping its wings for centuries. Whether it's the love of nature or the excitement of finding a rare bird, bird-watching never goes out of style. It's just for the birds, and that's perfectly fine.

11. When were birds used in mines for danger alerts, and were they divas about it?

Imagine yourself as a miner in the early 20th century. You're deep underground, chipping away at the earth. Your helmet light flickers, casting shadows around you. But there's a danger you can't see: carbon monoxide. This is where our hero, or rather, the diva, steps in—the canary.

Yes, these bright yellow birds were the original mine safety alarms, long before technology gave us gadgets. Starting in the late 1800s, miners took canaries into coal mines. Why? Their tiny size and fast metabolism made them super sensitive to toxic gases like carbon monoxide, sneaking through the tunnels.

But why canaries? Unlike your moody cat or the always-quiet goldfish, canaries have a flair for drama. Expose them to harmful gases, and they'd go silent or even fall from their perch. A clear, if unfortunate, warning. In short, they were the opera stars of the bird world: a bit over-the-top, but their dramatic performances could save lives.

This practice lasted a long time, only ending in Britain in 1986 when digital detectors took over. The canaries probably didn't mind leaving their risky job behind, but who knows? Maybe they missed their important role, even if it was a bit theatrical.

In the end, these singing miners earned a rightful place in history. They may not have worn hard hats, but their contribution was huge. A tale of wings and warning, proving that sometimes the smallest stars make the biggest impact.

12. When did birds first start flying, and what sparked this big change?

Imagine a world where birds are just really fancy, feathered dinosaurs trying to find their place in the prehistoric pecking order. It's about 150 million years ago during the Jurassic period—yes, the same time some dinosaurs were stomping around in their mighty, scaly splendor. Birds, or at least their ancestors, are strutting around, full of curiosity and maybe a touch of existential dread. Flying, it turns out, was just the next big leap.

But how did these ground-dwelling creatures take to the skies? It all started with some handy geological events and nature's clever tweaks. Birds' ancestors were small, two-legged dinosaurs with feathers. Yes, feathers—those fluffy things were originally meant to keep warm and perhaps to attract a mate during prehistoric dating games. Over time, some of these creatures started to grow something like wings. These proto-wings had an edge: they made gliding away from predators easier, catching snacks more fun, and simply moving around more stylish.

Transitioning from gliding to powered flight was a gradual shift. Picture a kid learning to ride a bike. At first, there's a lot of flapping and falling. Then, suddenly—flight! Archaeopteryx, a famous dino-bird, was one of these early fliers, paving the way for years of airborne antics.

The drive to fly was sparked by the age-old evolutionary rules of "eat-or-be-eaten" and "find-new-horizons." Flying opened up endless buffet choices, safer spots for nests, and views only the clouds knew.

So when you see birds soaring through the sky today, remember this—they're the high-fliers of a very exclusive club. Resourceful. Adaptable. Maybe a little showy, too. Evolution favors those willing to wing it—literally!

Myth Smashers

✘ MYTH:

Hummingbirds hitch rides on other birds to migrate.

✔ FACT:

Despite the charm of this myth, hummingbirds fly solo during migration. These small aviators are endurance champions, flying nonstop across vast distances without a helping wing.

✘ MYTH:

If you remove a bird from its nest, it won't survive.

✔ FACT:

Birds adapt quickly and can rebuild or relocate as needed. Like humans regrouping after a storm, birds assess their environment and adapt to ensure survival.

The HUHs

Birds sing after a storm; why shouldn't people feel as free to delight in whatever sunlight remains to them?

- John Webster

1. Huh?! Did you know some parrots have better rhythm than us, and do they wish for dance shows?

Parrots and rhythm? You bet! Some of our feathered friends might just have a leg—or wing—up on us when it comes to keeping a beat. Picture a parrot shimmying to Beyoncé or tapping its claws to rock and roll. It's a sight to see.

The world first danced to this tune thanks to a cockatoo named Snowball. He became an internet star with his slick moves to the Backstreet Boys' hit, "Everybody (Backstreet's Back)." Snowball wasn't just flapping about; he adjusted his moves to match the music's tempo. His rhythm was no accident.

But why can parrots groove so well? Unlike most animals, parrots are vocal learners. They have a natural gift for copying sounds, including human speech and music. Their brains are wired to link what they hear to their movements, likely because they evolved to mimic.

Do these talented parrots dream of dance shows? Well, we can't ask them directly (imagine the interviews!), but it seems they're just enjoying themselves. Parrots, like us, love fun and play.

So, next time you hit the dance floor, consider inviting a parrot. It might just outshine everyone with its moves! While they may not crave the spotlight at a theater, they're more than happy to keep the beat with their avian grooves.

2. Huh?! Did you know the European pied flycatcher plans for climate change, and should we take notes?

The European pied flycatcher, a tiny bird with a snazzy black-and-white outfit, seems to have taken a page from a survival guide for the future. This little creature, about the size of your palm, isn't just flitting around for fun. It's actually crafting a climate plan that could rival any big meeting of world leaders.

So, how does a bird plan for climate change? The flycatcher has a fantastic sense of timing. These birds rely on trees blossoming and a feast of insects to feed their chicks. But with warmer weather making springs arrive earlier, they've smartly adjusted their travel schedules. They're leaving their African winter homes sooner to catch the European spring food fest right when it's at its best. Talk about perfect timing!

This ability to change when they do things is due to something called phenological plasticity. A mouthful, right? Basically, it means these birds can change their activities based on what's happening around them. It's like setting your watch ahead for daylight saving time. But here, the stakes are much higher—it's about staying alive.

So, should we humans pay attention? Definitely! The flycatcher teaches us about being adaptable and thinking ahead. It shows us how important it is to be in tune with our environment. While we might not be able to wing it quite like these birds, we can certainly learn to be more flexible in changing times.

In the end, the European pied flycatcher isn't just a master of flying but also a smart planner for climate change. Next time you see one darting through the trees, think of it as a little reminder: staying ahead can mean the difference between just surviving and thriving. And who would have guessed birdwatching could be so full of lessons?

3. Huh?! Can you believe chickens are kin to T. rex, and do they feel the pressure?

Believe it or not, chickens are like little feathered reminders of the mighty Tyrannosaurus rex. While they might not roar or star in dinosaur movies, these cluckers have a surprising family tree. So, how did this link become common knowledge? And do chickens feel the weight of their prehistoric ancestors?

Thanks to the wonders of science and a bit of evolutionary storytelling, we know this connection. Scientists looked into the past using DNA studies and found out that birds are actually the closest living relatives to the dinosaurs. By comparing proteins found in fossils with those of modern birds, researchers discovered that the humble chicken shares more with T. rex than any other living creature. In the great family tree of life, chickens are just two branches away from the terrifying carnivore.

But do chickens feel this ancient connection? Let's be honest. If you've seen a chicken pecking around a farmyard, you'd probably say the closest they get to feeling the pressure is when they're laying an egg. Chickens are blissfully unaware of their famous ancestry. They're more interested in scratching for grains than thinking about their dino-dynasty.

In truth, chickens are quite happy leaving the roaring and tail-whipping to their Hollywood-rendered ancestors. So, while they may not feel the weight of their family tree, we humans can marvel at the fact that our breakfast egg layers are evolutionary cousins to the king of the prehistoric jungle.

This quirky connection is a fantastic reminder of the twists and turns of evolution. Next time you see a chicken, you might just picture it as a pocket-sized reminder. Birds have been ruling the roost for millions of years—long before there were even roosts to rule!

4. Huh?! Is it true pigeons know art styles, and are they secret critics?

Pigeons, those familiar city dwellers, may not be marching into art galleries with little berets and smart glasses, but they know a thing or two about art styles. Believe it or not, these birds have more up their feathers than just searching for bread crumbs.

Back in the 1990s, a clever psychologist named Shigeru Watanabe revealed something fascinating: pigeons can indeed tell apart different art styles. It's true! He trained pigeons using paintings by Monet and Picasso. The birds showed they could spot the difference between Impressionist and Cubist works, recognizing each style in their own birdy way. While they aren't exactly praising the brushwork or debating the emotional depth, they're definitely noticing patterns. Who knew?

How do they do it? Pigeons have amazing eyes. They see more colors than humans and notice tiny details we might miss. This super-vision helps them recognize different art styles. But as for their favorite—whether they're fans of Van Gogh's swirling skies over Cubist shapes—remains a mystery.

Think of pigeons as more of art historians than critics. They might not write reviews in bird journals, but they sure know how to organize art by its looks. So next time, if you catch a pigeon eyeing a street mural, it's not pondering deep thoughts; it's just admiring the colors and patterns. Strange but true, in the quirky world of pigeons and paint, even birds can appreciate a good brushstroke!

5. Huh?! Did you know some birds "borrow" nests, and are they bad decorators?

You might think birds are nature's builders, weaving twigs and leaves into cozy nests every season. But not all birds are competing for "Best Nest" awards. Some, like cuckoos and cowbirds, are more into Airbnb than DIY. They don't just borrow nests; they sneak their eggs into other birds' nests, much like leaving a baby at daycare without a heads-up. This little trick is called brood parasitism, and it's as if your neighbor always borrows your lawnmower and forgets to return it.

Now, are these feathered freeloaders bad decorators? Not quite. They're more like house guests who never bother with chores. Instead, they rely on their unsuspecting hosts to do all the hard work. The host birds, perhaps not big fans of home improvement shows, end up raising these intruder chicks as if they were their own. It's a genius move, letting cuckoos and cowbirds fly carefree, leaving the decorating to others.

This "rent-free" lifestyle might seem cheeky, but it's a smart evolutionary game plan. By outsourcing parenting, these birds can focus on what they do best—finding food and making more baby birds. It's like skipping housework to chase your dreams, but with more strategy.

So, next time you see a bird's nest, remember: it might not be poor decorating skills at play. It could be a sign of clever bird strategy. A bird-eat-bird world, indeed, where these cheeky birds are living their best lives—one borrowed nest at a time!

6. Huh?! Did you know some birds sleep with one eye open, and do they dream of flying?

Imagine a world where you could nap while keeping half an eye on Netflix, ready to pause whenever something exciting happens. Some birds are the masters of this trick, sleeping with one eye open. This clever habit is called "unihemispheric slow-wave sleep." It lets birds rest one side of their brain while the other stays on guard. Nature's way of saying, "Sleep tight, but don't let the predators bite."

But do birds dream of flying? Scientists aren't sure if birds are replaying their latest sky dance or planning new tricks in their dreams. However, some research hints that birds might indeed dream. How come? They experience REM sleep, just like us humans, which is when we tend to dream.

Take the zebra finch, for example. Studies show that these little guys might practice their songs in their sleep, like dreaming of their own karaoke contest. So, if finches are dreaming of hitting the right notes, maybe other birds are dreaming of catching that perfect wind or that juicy worm that got away.

In the end, while we humans might dream of flying, birds might keep their dreams a bit more real—or maybe not; nature is always full of surprises. Until we can peek into their dreams, we can only guess what birds think of during their naps. Next time you see a bird resting, give it a nod—it might just be dreaming up its next big adventure!

7. Huh?! Can you believe there's a bird that copies human laughter, and do they join in jokes?

There's a bird out there that might just make you think your jokes hit across species! Meet the lyrebird, a fantastic mimic from Australia's forests. This feathered impressionist can copy a wide range of sounds, from chainsaws to camera clicks and, yes, even human laughter.

The secret to the lyrebird's mimicry is its complex syrinx, a special voice box that lets it create an amazing mix of sounds with pinpoint accuracy. While they might not be chuckling at your knock-knock jokes, their imitation of laughter is often so spot-on that you'd swear they were in on the joke. This skill likely evolved to impress mates and scare off predators, but it sure does make for some entertaining run-ins with us humans.

Though they don't get the punchline, these birds show us the playful brainpower of the animal kingdom. So, the next time you hear unexpected giggles in the woods, it could be a lyrebird perfecting its comedy act. The real kicker? Nature keeps astounding us with its talents, making us wonder if one day, a lyrebird might just join us at a comedy club!

WHY WHAT HUH?!

8. Huh?! Did you know crows have funerals, and should we invite them to ours?

Crows, those black-feathered creatures that once starred in Hitchcock movies, have a surprisingly complex social life. They even hold what can only be described as funerals. Yes, when a crow hits the ground and meets its end, a group of fellow crows gathers around, cawing loudly in what looks like a bird version of a memorial service.

But why do they do this? Scientists have some ideas. One thought is that crows are having a kind of learning session—like a detective meeting to solve a mystery. By examining the scene where their pal died, they might pick up tips to avoid the same fate. Another idea is that they're showing respect, a behavior seen in creatures with complex social networks. It's like a tiny bird funeral, just without the flower arrangements and cake.

Should we invite crows to our funerals? It's an interesting idea. Picture the scene: Aunt Edna, Uncle Joe, and a bunch of crows perched nearby. They'd probably enjoy the drama but might give Aunt Edna a start with their loud calls and intense stares. On the plus side, they wouldn't gossip about the floral displays or mention how long the speeches are.

In short, while crow funerals aren't the quiet events we humans know, they offer a fascinating glimpse into animal social life. So, should you send a crow an invite to your next family event? Maybe, just to add some unexpected fun to the day. Who knew these black birds were masters of both intrigue and etiquette?

9. Huh?! Is it true some birds use ants as a spa treatment, and are they getting a free scrub?

The bird world has its very own spa day, featuring an unlikely helper: the ant. Yes, some clever birds have figured out a way to enjoy a spa treatment by letting ants crawl all over their feathers. This strange behavior, called "anting," turns ants into little cleaning machines.

Why would birds voluntarily host an ant parade on their feathers? It's not just for fun. These birds are getting more than a tickly sensation; they're enjoying a free pest-control service. Many ants produce something called formic acid when threatened. This natural chemical helps birds get rid of annoying parasites. Imagine a bird bath where, instead of water, ants do all the work—offering both a cleansing rinse and a feather conditioner.

Scientists are still puzzling over all the benefits birds get from anting, but the list keeps growing. It might help with fungus, bacteria, and even soothe itchy skin. Birds seem thrilled with this arrangement, often picking up ants and running them through their feathers like they're getting a fancy hair treatment.

Don't rush to break up an anting session if you spot one. Instead, admire the bird's ingenuity. Nature is providing a free spa day—no booking required. Birds have truly nailed the art of living well without spending a dime.

10. Huh?! Did you know pigeons were war heroes, and do they have tiny medals?

Pigeons as war heroes might sound like a wild story, but it's a real feathered fact. Imagine this: in the middle of war chaos, when radios failed, it was pigeons that soared with important messages. These bird warriors flew into history, doing their bit with every coo and flap of their wings.

During both World Wars, pigeons played big parts. They carried messages over enemy lines when other ways didn't work. Their trustworthiness was so high that they got sent with key notes tied to their legs. One famous pigeon, Cher Ami, even saved almost 200 American soldiers in World War I by delivering a note that stopped an attack on their own troops. This brave bird earned the Croix de Guerre, a top French award for courage. It wasn't a tiny medal, but it was a huge honor.

And pigeons aren't alone in animal military service. Dogs have sniffed out danger, dolphins have found underwater bombs, and even cats were thought about for secret missions—though they were a bit too independent for the job.

While pigeons don't wear little medals, they've been honored in other ways. The British PDSA Dickin Medal, often called the animal version of the Victoria Cross, has gone to a few famous pigeons. So, even without fancy bling, they're remembered as brave birds who changed history with their flights.

Next time you spot a pigeon pecking crumbs in the park, give a nod of respect. That simple bird might just be a descendant of one of those war heroes. Who knew pigeons had such a cool history?

11. Huh?! Did you know some birds see magnetic fields, and are we missing something?

Imagine a world where you have a superpower that lets you see magnetic fields. Think of it as being a kind of superhero—like a pigeon! Yes, some birds have this nifty ability called magnetoreception. They see the Earth's magnetic field, guiding them like a hidden compass. Picture them in tiny capes, flying with purpose.

So, how do they pull off this magical feat? The secret lies in certain proteins in their eyes called cryptochromes. These little guys react to the Earth's magnetic field, giving our feathery pals a sort of built-in navigation system. No need for Google Maps here. Imagine having the ultimate biological GPS!

While we're busy fumbling with compasses and GPS, birds, like robins and pigeons, simply rely on their "Sixth Sense". Not the spooky movie one, but one of nature's clever tricks. It's evolution's gift, allowing them to travel miles without getting lost. And it's a gift we humans might secretly envy.

Are we missing out? Not really. More like never got the chance. Instead, humans have our own tricks. We invent stuff to mimic nature's wonders. Our brains are wired for creativity and invention. We crack the puzzle of direction with gadgets and tech. So, we might not "see" magnetic fields, but we've sent a Tesla to space!

In the end, it's not about missing out. It's about marveling at nature's quirks and using our own kind of magic to understand them. Next time you see a bird flying straight and true, give a little nod. These natural navigators have their magnetic powers, and who knew bird watching could be so... electrifying?

12. Huh?! Did you know the lyrebird copies construction sounds, and are they adding to urban noise?

Picture this: you're wandering through a peaceful forest when suddenly you hear... a jackhammer? Your ears might think they've strolled onto a building site, but don't worry—it's likely just the lyrebird putting on its show. This Australian bird is a master mimic, and it's got quite the repertoire. It can mimic other birds, sure, but it doesn't stop there. How about chainsaws and camera clicks? Yup, it can do those too.

The lyrebird's talent would make any comedian jealous. It doesn't just mimic animal sounds; it takes on the noise of the modern world. In areas where nature and cities blend, these birds pick up on the sounds around them. Construction tools, car alarms, even the latest smartphone ringtone—it's all fair game.

Now, you might wonder, is the lyrebird adding to the urban noise problem? Not really. These birds are more like that quirky sound clip you hear every now and then, not the main noise culprits. They're tiny sound bites in the big city symphony. Their mimicry shows how animals adapt to our ever-changing world in amazing ways.

And there's more to their mimicry than just making noise. In the wild, male lyrebirds use their sound skills to impress the ladies. Their performance is a way to show off their skills and prove their patch of forest is safe and sound.

So, while the lyrebird's tunes are entertaining, they're not exactly causing noise pollution. They remind us of the incredible ways nature and humans interact. Next time you think you hear construction in the wilderness, stop and listen. It could be a lyrebird inviting you to its unique concert. When nature's DJ hits play, it's a show you don't want to miss!

Myth Smashers

✖ MYTH:

Bread is good food for birds.

✓ FACT:

Bread lacks essential nutrients birds need to thrive. Feeding birds bread is akin to a diet of only carbs for humans—there's a balance to be maintained for health.

✖ MYTH:

Birds' feet will freeze to metal perches.

✓ FACT:

Birds have unique circulation in their feet that prevents freezing, even on cold metal. It's like wearing thermal socks that preserve heat efficiently on chilly mornings.

WHY WHAT HUH?!

Made in the USA
Monee, IL
28 January 2025